PETERHOF

ORANIENBAUM · S

GOLDEN
LION

The History of Peterhof

PETERHOF... the Pearl of the Baltic, the capital of fountains. An astonishing place, where majestic architecture, stone and bronze, splashing water and magnificent landscapes celebrate the triumph of beauty and the joy of life.

"Peterhof is often compared with Versailles, but that is a misunderstanding," Alexander Benois, a passionate admirer of the residence, remarked. "Peterhof gets an absolutely unique character from the sea. Peterhof

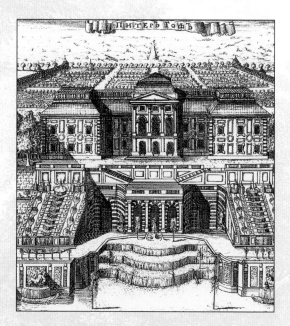

The Great Cascade and the Upper Chambers. Engraving by Alexei Rostovtsev. 1717

Portrait of Peter I. Artist: Benoit Coffre. 1716

was born, as it were, from sea-foam, as if summoned into life at the behest of the mighty king of the seas ..."

In 1705 Peter I, the future "king of the seas", was sailing in his snow (two-masted ship) *Munker* along the south shore of the Gulf of Finland, newly recovered from the Swedes, when with his characteristic far-sightedness he noted the enchanting beauty of these parts. The Tsar ordered that a small manor with a wooden house and service buildings be constructed here. This was the beginning of his beloved Peterhof, which means in German "Peter's court". Here the Tsar, who was constantly on the move, stopped to rest during his frequent journeys to the fortifications being built on and around the

island of Kotlin, a vital outpost to defend recently founded St Petersburg.

In 1712 St Petersburg became the capital of Russia. The young city was to rival the best metropolises in Europe and its founder – an eternal romantic – was already possessed with the idea of surrounding his "paradise" with a string of summer residences. Chief among them was Peterhof on the coast.

In early August 1720 Peter personally inspected the springs situated at a height of 70–100 metres on the northern slopes of the Ropsha Heights, some 20 kilometres to the south of Peterhof. The decision that immediately followed to construct a canal along which this water would be brought to Peterhof by gravity ensured the future of the estate's fountains. On 8 August 1721 the Ropsha canal was formally opened and just

View of the Great Palace and Great Cascade. Artist: Ivan Aivazovsky. 1837

View of the Italian Fountain in the Lower Park at Peterhof. Engraving by Stepan Galaktionov after a drawing by Silvester Shchedrin. 1804–05

sir and the Hermitage. This became the basis for the design of the Lower Park with its palaces, pavilions, cascades and fountains.

Peter I was exceptionally fortunate: few people manage to come up with such a grand idea and see it realized in their own lifetime. The founder of Peterhof was one of them and he left his dream come true for posterity.

The next phase in the evolution of Peterhof is associated with the reign of Peter's daughter, Empress Elizabeth. This was the heyday of the Baroque style with its love of striking vistas, theatrical effects and imposing spaces. It was in this style that the architect Francesco Bartolomeo Rastrelli enlarged the Upper Chambers into the Great Palace, one of his finest creations.

The second major builder of Peterhof after Peter I is considered to be Emperor Nicholas I. His 30-year reign took the residence to new heights. He made the improvement of Peterhof an important part of his life. The glistening splendour of the Lower Park was less to Nicholas's taste – he preferred the quiet attractions of the semi-neglected area adjoining it on the east. There he not only constructed a family home, but in-

a few hours later water spurted in silvery jets from Peterhof's first fountains. These installations were a physical expression of Peter's love for the watery element and, although he lacked training in this field, the Tsar himself often found the best solutions for construction that were then approved by specialists. A number of his own drawings that established the basic layout of the residence still survive. On one of them we find three diverging rays – the Sea Canal and the alleys running from the "Upper Chambers" to Monplai-

View of the Great Palace at Oranienbaum from the Courtyard. Artist: Friedrich Hartmann Barisien. 1758

View of Tsarina's Island. Lithograph by Carl Schultz after a drawing by Johann Meyer. Circa 1845

stituted a distinctive way of life. This estate, Nicholas's brainchild, was created for his beloved wife. Alexandra Feodorovna, and was named in her honour: "Her Imperial Majesty's Own Dacha Alexandria". The Emperor was personally involved in the creation of its palaces and parks. Alexandria is also connected with the family life of the last Russian Emperor, Nicholas II. In his reign Peterhof became practically the capital of the country in the summer months and four of his five children were born here.

Peterhof today

PETERHOF remains as it has always been an exceptional place. The ensemble of buildings gradually evolved, becoming a sort of encyclopaedia of architectural styles and artistic tastes, a reflection of three centuries in the history of Russia.

After the 1917 revolution the palaces and parks of Peterhof were nationalized and soon opened as museums that operated successfully until the Nazi invasion in the summer of 1941. After stubborn fighting in September 1941 Soviet forces were obliged to leave Peterhof and until January 1944 the town and all its museum facilities were occupied by the invaders. In that time seemingly irreparable damage was inflicted on the buildings and grounds of the complex. The post-war recreation of Peterhof was one of the great feats of the Leningrad school of restoration. Hundreds of people worked to return the Great Palace to life under the guidance of the architects Vasily Savkov and Yevgenia Kazanskaya. As early as the summer of 1946 the grand inauguration the first 38 restored fountains took place. A year later the looted Samson returned to his place, created anew by the sculptor Vasily Simonov. Then more restored fountains gradually opened along with

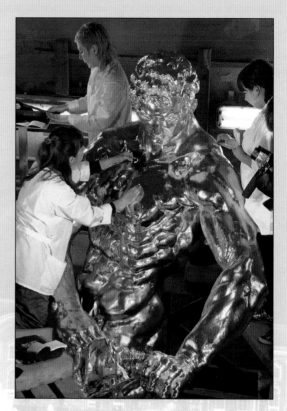

Samson being regilded in the workshop

Festivals at Peterhof

Festivals at Peterhof

museum have gained the approval of our colleagues: in 2011 the Peterhof State Museum-Preserve was awarded the prestigious Museum Olympus prize of the Inter-departmental Museum Council in the Museum of the Year category.

At the same time Peterhof has retained its principles and traditions. The monuments of various eras created in the capital of fountains since the time of Peter the Great are kept in superb condition. The splendour of Peterhof remains a symbol of Russia statehood, a symbol of our country's greatness.

the revived palace-museums. Restoration work has been continuing at Peterhof for decades. The latest stage was completed in the summer of 2011 with the opening of the Church Pavilion of the Great Palace museum in the recreated interior of the Church of the Apostles Peter and Paul. All this time the collections have been enlarged, palaces have been opened and new museums created. A significant role in the development of the complex was played by the collecting activities of Vadim Znamenov, who for over 30 years was head of the staff of the museum-preserve.

Recent years have seen a new stage in the life of Peterhof. Today the museum-preserve is engaged in the restoration of the palaces and parks of Oranienbaum, which in 2007 became part of the museum complex. To mark the 300th anniversary of Oranienbaum the Great Menshikov and Chinese Palaces opened their doors to visitors. The Alexandria Park continues to develop into a family leisure facility. In 2010 the Farm Palace opened there, followed in 2011 by the Imperial Telegraph Office. In the Lower Park there has been a major restoration of the sculpture of the Great Cascade and in the spring of 2011 the regilded centrepiece – *Samson Tearing Apart the Jaws of the Lion* – made a second journey through the streets of St Petersburg, in part retracing its post-war route.

The unique *son et lumière* events focussed on the Great Cascade have acquired a new look. Their modern format exploiting multimedia technologies draws thousands of spectators. Peterhof was one of the first cultural sites in Russia to be included in the *Google Maps* system, adding still more to its popularity and visitor numbers. The innovations in the life of the Peterhof

Upper Garden

THE MAGNIFICENT Baroque ensemble of the Upper Garden is a striking example of the regular style of garden design. A strict geometrical layout, trees and bushed trimmed into elaborate shapes, fountains, a host of decorative sculpture and flowerbeds – all of this seems a sort of continuation of the gilded halls of the palace.

The decoration of the Upper Garden dates from the middle of the 18th century. Under Peter I this area had a practical function. It contained a garden where vegetables and medicinal herbs were grown for the court and ponds where fish were bred. The first fountains appeared here in the 1730s to the design of the architects Johann Blank and Ivan Davydov and the fountain engineer Paul Sualem. The basins were adorned by elaborate

lead sculptural compositions created by Carlo Bartolomeo Rastrelli. The decoration of the fountains changed repeatedly over the years but the general composition of the garden remained the same. In the 19th century, in keeping with the new fashion for landscape parks with a natural look, the gardeners stopped trimming the trees in the Upper Garden. The area retained its regularity only in the layout and the Baroque fountains.

During the Second World War the Upper Garden was seriously harmed: a large anti-tank ditch was dug across the centre; many trees perished and the water conduits were damaged. The post-war restoration returned the Upper Garden to its full "regular" appearance and now it is a superb example of the "French" style of landscape design.

The Indeterminate Fountain

THE UNUSUAL NAME of the southernmost fountain in the Upper Garden is most likely a result of repeated changes of decoration. After the war it was given back its Baroque character, with bronze figures of four dolphins and a dragon being installed in the basin. The fountain is situated close to the entrance to the Upper Garden, which is flanked by grand pillars from the middle of the 18th century.

The Main Gates of the Upper Garden

The Apollo Cascade

BY THE SOUTHERN edge of the basin of the *Neptune* fountain, on a platform paved in marble with a checkerboard pattern and washed by two miniature fountains, stands a bronze copy of the ancient Apollo Belvedere, the famous creation of Leochares. This small ensemble is known as the Apollo Cascade. Original the place of the Greek god was occupied by a statue of *Winter*. That was replaced in 1800 by the figure of Apollo cast in the Academy of Arts by Vasily Yakimov.

Riders on hippocampi. Detail of the *Neptune* fountain

The Neptune Fountain

THE CENTRAL PLACE in the composition of the Upper Garden is allotted to the Neptune Fountain. In the mid-1700s the basin was adorned by a multi-figure lead composition of Neptune's chariot, intended to stress the maritime character of the residence. The dilapidated sculpture soon had to be removed, but the idea of a fountain dedicated to the god of the sea remained. After Paul I came to the throne, the *Neptune* sculptural group that he had acquired in Nuremberg was brought to Peterhof. It is noteworthy for having been cast in the 1650s, making it the oldest work of sculpture in the Peterhof parks. After its installation in the Upper Garden in 1799, the composition became the key element of this whole area, a hymn to Russia gaining access to the Baltic under Peter the Great.

Statues of *Vertumnus* and *Zephyr*. Sculptor: Antonio Bonazza. 1757

The Oak Fountain

THIS FOUNTAIN was constructed on the central axis of the Upper Garden in front of the Great Palace. The round basin contains a six-pointed tufa-limestone star around the edges of which are spouting figures of dolphins. In the centre is a statue of *Cupid with a Theatrical Mask* (1809) by Giacomo Rossi. The name of this fountain refers back to its decoration in the 18th century, when a lead oak-tree stood in the basin. Next to the fountain are four marble statues by the well-known sculptor Antonio Bonazza (the son of Giovanni Bonazza, the creator of *Adam* and *Eve* in the Lower Park).

The Square Ponds Fountains

The Western Square Pond

THE WESTERN AND EASTERN "Square" Ponds are placed symmetrically in front of the galleries of the Great Palace. They were dug out in Peter I's time to serve as reservoirs of water for the fountain system. Later a fountain was installed in the centre of each. Still today these reservoirs that feed the jets in the central part of the Lower Park remain an adornment of the Upper Garden thanks to their marble statues surrounded by bronze dolphins and low-rise jets of water.

The statue of the *Venus Italica* in the centre of the fountain in the Western Square Pond. After an original by Antonio Canova. 1812

The statue of *Apollino* in the centre of the fountain in the Eastern Square Pond. After an original by the school of Praxiteles. 4th century BC

The Eastern Square Pond

A tunnel of greenery

The Great Palace

EUROPEAN palace-and-park ensembles traditionally served not only as places of residence for monarchs, but also as a means of singing their praises. The Great Palace was from the outset perceived as central to the message the Peterhof ensemble. Peter entrusted the construction of the original Upper Chambers or Palace on the Hill to Johann Friedrich Braunstein, who made a building on the high natural terrace with a view of the sea – the main "war trophy" of Peterhof's founder. In 1714 work began on the Sea Canal, running from the palace to the Gulf of Finland. Vessels would enter the canal, moor along its banks and the guests would

continue on foot to the palace. Empress Elizabeth resolved to give her father's residence a grander appearance. In reconstructing the palace, her architect, Francesco Bartolomeo Rastrelli, took a very conservative attitude to the existing building and preserved its general composition and its central part. Success was guaranteed by Rastrelli's loving respect for every detail created by Peter's will. In the hands of the great master the building acquired a monumental, yet exquisite appearance. The overall length of the façade that it turns to the sea was now around 300 metres.

An Allegory
of Spring.
After a drawing
by Francesco
Bartolomeo
Rastrelli.
1749–51

The Main Staircase

THE STAIRCASE occupies part of a wing specially built by Rastrelli that adjoins the main body of the palace at right-angles on the side of the Upper Garden. Here Rastrelli created by 1755 a life-affirming Baroque hymn of praise to the rule of Peter I's daughter, Empress Elizabeth. This 12-metre high interior is stunning for its gleaming gilding and expressive decoration. The impression of soaring height is enhanced by the ceiling painting, a work by Bartolomeo Tarsia showing the goddess Flora dashing through the clouds in a chariot generously scattering white flower. The walls, window embrasures and coving are decorated with rich ornamental painting (by Antonio Peresinotti). The sumptuous surround to the door into the Ballroom is topped by a crown and allegorical figures of Truth and Mercy. In niches and on the pedestals of the stair-rail are gilded allegorical figures of the seasons. The elegance of the staircase is underlined by the partly gilded wrought-iron panels of the balustrade forged by N. Stube.

The Ballroom

THE BALLROOM is one of the most brilliant interiors created by Francesco Bartolomeo Rastrelli. It has a floor area of 270 square metres (2,900 sq. ft) but seems considerably larger due to the high vault, mirrors and large two-tier windows. The abundance of gilding creates the impression of particular grandeur and brilliance.

Tondo: *The Rape of Europe*. Artist: Giuseppe Valeriani. 1740s

Broad, elaborately shaped and painted coving frames a gigantic painting that occupies the full area of the ceiling – *Mount Parnassus*, created in 1751 by Bartolomeo Tarsia and featuring Empress Elizabeth in the guise of Juno. On the walls and between the windows are 16 painted tondi by Giuseppe Valeriani on subjects from Ovid's *Metamorphoses* and Virgil's *Aeneid*.

Tondo: *Hera and Cupid*. Artist: Giuseppe Valeriani. 1740s

The Blue Reception Room

RASTRELLI decorated this smaller interior in a comparatively modest manner in keeping with its service function: this was a place of work for secretaries and the officials who kept the journals that recorded events in the life of the court. The walls are lined with a light blue damask that gave the room its name, while the panels, window frames and doors are embellished with gilded carving. This décor is harmoniously complemented by a patterned parquet floor, a multi-tiered heating stove covered with blue-and-white tiles and a ceiling painting, *An Allegory of Glory*, by an unknown 18th-century artist, as well as the elegant furniture and bronze and porcelain articles that were executed in the 19th century in the "Second Rococo" style. The room contains three painted views of Peterhof, one of them by the outstanding seascape artist Ivan Aivazovsky.

The Loss of a Russian Ship. Artist: Jacob Philipp Hackert. 1771

Decorative vase. Imperial Porcelain
Factory, St Petersburg, Russia.
Circa 1830

The Chesme Hall

THE CHESME HALL is a remarkable memorial to Russia's naval triumphs in the second half of the 18th century. It was designed in the 1770s on the orders of Catherine II by Yury Veldten, who used stucco moulding (by the craftsmen Nasonov and Bernasconi) in the decoration. All the décor of the hall served to extol Russia as a naval power that defeated Turkey in the struggle for supremacy in the Black Sea: portraits of ancient heroes and symbols of triumph, the ceiling painting *The Sacrifice of Iphigenia* (one of the episodes leading up to the Trojan War) by Augustin Terwesten the Elder, Turkish weapons, sultans and crescents representing the defeated enemy. The chief adornment of the hall is twelve large canvases painted in 1771–73 by the German artist Jacob Philipp Hackert. Six of them present episodes from the famous Battle of Chesme (1770), in which the Russian fleet commanded by Count Alexei Orlov inflicted a crushing defeat on the Ottoman navy.

Portrait of Alexei Orlov. Sculptor: Giovanni Antonio Cibei. 1770s

The Throne Room

THE THRONE ROOM is the largest hall in the palace (330 square metres, 3,500 sq. ft). It was designed by Rastrelli for official receptions, concerts and balls. In 1777 Catherine II had it redecorated by Veldten. His project was founded on the idea of statehood, the theme of civic duty and service to one's country. The hall is striking for the abundance of light and air and the harmoniousness of the decoration. A background of cold green walls embellished with stucco ornament and reliefs by Ivan Prokofiev, Mikhail Kozlovsky and Arkhip Ivanov effectively sets off the portraits of members of the Romanov dynasty. The place above the throne is

Relief: *Justice.*
Sculptor: Ivan Prokofiev.
1770s

The throne
in the Throne Room.
Early 18th century

taken by an equestrian portrait of Catherine II (1762) painted by the Danish artist Vigilius Erichsen specially for this hall. On the western wall are four works depicting the Battle of Chesme by the English artist Richard Paton. The throne here was, according to tradition, made for Peter I to a commission from his closest associate, Prince Alexander Menshikov. It is made of carved oak, gilded and upholstered with red velvet.

The Audience Hall
(Room for Ladies-in-Waiting)

Sculpture: *Pastoral Scene*. From a model by Johann Joachim Kändler. Meissen Porcelain factory, Saxony, Germany

THIS HALL, intended as a setting for audiences, is another of Rastrelli's masterpieces. The play of light in the many mirrors, the gilded windings of the woodcarving and the bright ceiling painting by the Italian Paolo Ballarini combine to produce an impression of refined luxury. On "Kurtäge", days when the palace hosted gatherings of the nobility, the hall turned into a reception room. Still today, card-tables from the mid-1700s stand around its walls. Also on display here is a splendid collection of Meissen porcelain.

The White Dining-Room

THIS BRIGHT spacious interior created by Yury Veldten for Catherine II delights the eye with the elegance of its exquisite stuccowork executed by Russian craftsmen under the direction of the specialist Bernasconi. Oval medallions on the upper part of the walls contain scenes from the ancient myth of Dionysus and Ariadne (sculptor: Feodor Gordeyev). The large table is set with a service for 30 persons that was commissioned by Catherine II from the outstanding English potter Josiah Wedgwood and made at his Etruria works in 1768. The crystal chandeliers and girandoles were produced by the St Petersburg Glassworks in the 1760s and 1770s.

Panel: *Cupids Holding Up a Basket of Fruit*

Items from a table service. Made by Josiah Wedgwood, Etruria works, England. 1760s

Figure of a pheasant. China.
Second half of the 17th century

The Eastern Chinese Cabinet

The Chinese Cabinets

IN THE LATE 1760s two Chinese cabinets were created by the architect Jean-Baptiste Vallin de La Mothe on either side of the Picture Hall, the central room in the Great Palace. The walls are lined with damask, yellow in the western cabinet, crimson in the eastern one. Decoration of these rooms in a Chinese style was a tribute to a fashion first introduced in Russia by Peter the Great. The walls are adorned with panels from old Chinese screens painted in gold and silver on a black lacquer background (two are original, the rest recreated). An impression of exceptional decorativeness is produced by the fanciful painting around the windows, on the panels, doors and ceilings, the elaborate stoves with polychrome tiles and the parquet floors assembled from precious varieties of wood. The cabinets house a collection of Chinese and Japanese porcelain of the 18th and 19th centuries, enamels, and richly inlaid furniture.

The Western Chinese Cabinet

The Picture Hall

Detail of the decoration of the western wall with portraits by Pietro Rotari

THE ROOM, of which Friedrich Wilhelm von Bergholtz, a member of the visiting Duke of Holstein-Gottorp's suite, wrote "a magnificent hall, whence a splendid view of the see opens up and one can make out St Petersburg, in the distance to the right, and slightly to the left Kronslot," was the heart of Peter I's Upper Chambers. After Rastrelli's reconstruction it was the last in the suite of state rooms. Originally the hall was known as the Italian Salon. Its walls were hung with tapestries and paintings by Dutch and Flemish artists. Still left from Peter's time are the moulded frieze, the painting on the coving and the ceiling painting – *The History of Hieroglyphics* (1726) by Bartolomeo Tarsia. In the mid-1700s Rastrelli added to the décor mirrors, a parquet with an eye-catching diamond pattern and gilded woodcarving. All this combines happily with the paintings in the Rococo style by the Italian artist Pietro Rotari. They were placed on the walls "tapestry-fashion" (with no gaps between) in 1764 in an arrangement by the architect Vallin de La Mothe.

The Partridge Room (Boudoir)

THIS ELEGANT boudoir was created by Yury Veldten in the 1770s in the oldest, Petrine part of the palace. Its architectural focus is the partition containing the niche for a divan. It is decorated with gilded woodcarving which has an elegant lightness about it that gives the room a pleasantly intimate atmosphere. The room's colour scheme is based on a combination of light blue, white, greenish and golden tones. The same colours predominate in the pattern of the silk depicting partridges amongst flowers that was used to line the walls. It was created by the outstanding French artist and designer Philippe de Lasalle, known for his splendid fabrics.

The Partridge Room (Boudoir)

The Divan Room

THE STATE BEDCHAMBER created in the first half of the 18th century was later divided by a wooden partition with an alcove for the Empress's bed. In the 1770s Yury Veldten redesigned this room. It got its new name after a massive Turkish divan, said to be a war trophy, was installed

The Divan Room

Sculpture of Catherine II's pet dog Zemira. From a model by Jacques Dominique Rachette. Imperial Porcelain Factory, St Petersburg, Russia. 1779

here. Grigory Potemkin acquired this impressive piece of furniture directly from the theatre of war and presented it to Catherine II. After victory in the Russo-Turkish War there was a vogue in St Petersburg for huge divans that filled the drawing-rooms of the aristocracy and were known as "Potemkin divans".

The Dressing Room

Clock. Imperial Porcelain Factory, St Petersburg, Russia. 1843

The Study

THE STUDY that ends the suite of private rooms is lined with a light-coloured silk with floral ornaments. The décor in Rastrelli's traditional manner did not accord well with the name of the room and most probably gave it a certain piquancy characteristic of a place conducive to conversation and frivolous pastimes. The daily need for the Empress to concern herself with the affairs of state is demonstrated by the desk with writing implements.

The Study

The Dressing Room

THE COSY Dressing Room has retained the imprint of Rastrelli's style. The walls are lined with an ornate silk featuring bouquets framed with garlands of flowers that was woven in the 1840s at the Sapozhnikov brothers' factory. In the 19th century that factory was unrivalled in Russia for the dimensions and quality of the brocades and silks it produced. The room is enhanced by fine furniture, works of decorative art and portraits of crowned owners of the Great Palace.

The Passage or Standard Room

IN THE 18th century this was a passage room; in the 19th it became the Standard Room as it was the place where the standards of the regiments guarding the residence were kept. Here, as in the Dressing Room and Study the same silk fabric has been used on the walls and the furniture – a typical feature of Russian interiors in the middle and second half of the

The Passage or Standard Room

Card table.
Made by
Nikifor
Vasilyev.
1770s

serf artist belonging to Count Sheremetev. Alongside are portraits of the couple's daughter, Empress Elizabeth (by an unknown 18th-century artist) and Catherine II (a replica of the famous 1769 portrait by the remarkable Russian artist Feodor Rokotov).

A special role in the decoration of this interior is played by the furniture, notably the light elegant armchairs adorned with carved and gilded ornament and a splendid Russian-made folding card-table featuring architectural landscapes skilfully executed in the marquetry technique by Nikifor Vasilyev.

The Cavaliers' Room

18th century. The colours of the silk – bright green with rocaille ornament and bouquets of flowers – superbly sets off the gilded carving of the door surrounds that were executed to Rastrelli's designs and gives the room an elevated smartness and cheerfulness. The upbeat character of the interior is enhanced by the portraits hung here. There is an allegorical depiction of Peter the Great with the goddess of wisdom Minerva, painted in London in the 1730s by the Venetian artist Jacopo Amiconi to a commission from Prince Antioch Cantemir, and a portrait of Peter's wife, Catherine I, by an unknown

The Apotheosis of War. Unknown artist of the school of Rubens.
Second half of the 17th century

Portrait of Vittoria
Accoramboni. Artist:
Scipione Pulzone. 1570s

Clock. France. First half
of the 18th century

The Small Passage Room

The Cavaliers' Room

IMMEDIATELY adjoining the apartments of
the emperors and empresses was the guardroom
used by the elite Cavalier Guards responsible for
their personal security. Gentlemen of the court
and senior Guards officers would await an audi-
ence in this room designed by Rastrelli. Particularly striking here are the door surrounds richly
decorated with gilded wood carving. The walls
are lined with dark crimson damask and hung
with paintings by Western European artist of the
second half of the 17th century.

The Small Passage Room

THIS TINY ROOM is adorned by a light-
coloured silk with an elegant floral pattern. The
fabric was woven in the mid-19th century at the
Sapozhnikovs' factory specially for Peterhof. On
the walls are paintings, most notably *The Apotheosis of War*, created in the studio of the great
Flemish artist Peter Paul Rubens. His style is
typified by monumental forms, theatrical composition and a bright colour scheme.

The Large (Blue) Drawing-Room

THE BLUE DRAWING-ROOM was created by Rastrelli during the reconstruction of the Upper Chambers. The "standard" gilded wood carving combines wonderfully here with the painted decoration of the coving by the Russian artist Login Doritsky. The painting skilfully incorporates Empress Elizabeth's monogram, military symbols, banners and plant ornaments. The pale blue silk on the walls sets off formal portraits of Catherine II and Maria Feodorovna, the wife of Emperor Paul I. This room was used for formal lunches and dinners, for which in the 19th-century reign of Nicholas I the magnificent Banquet Service for 250 persons with over 5,000 pieces was created.

Candelabrum. Saxony. 1850s

The dessert section of the Banquet Service

Catherine II as Legislatrix in the Temple of Themis. Unknown late 18th-century artist after a 1783 original by Dmitry Levitsky

Chandelier. 1851

The Secretary's Room or Choir Anteroom

THE SECOND name for this small service room comes from its position next to the choir galleries of the Palace Church. A door from the Secretary's Room leads onto the eastern gallery and from there into the church itself. The decoration of the room was carried out in the mid-1700s to Rastrelli's designs. The post-war restorers recreated the zigzag parquet floor typical of the architect, restored the carved panels, the gilded window embrasures, the tiled stove and also the stylish silk on the walls. The interior is adorned by some splendid pieces created at the Imperial Porcelain Factory in the middle of the 19th century – a chandelier for 48 candles and decorative vases with ormolu mounts.

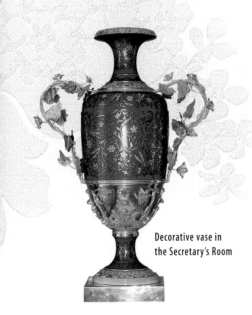

Decorative vase in the Secretary's Room

Sculpture: Lady in 18th-Century Costume. After a model by August Spies. Imperial Porcelain Factory, Russia

The first room of the Spare Apartment

The Rooms of the Spare Apartment

FROM THE NORTHERN enfilade guests entered "Olga's Apartment" that was created by the architect Andrei Stakenschneider in 1846 for the marriage of Grand Duchess Olga, the middle daughter of Nicholas I. These rooms occupied the interior of the east wing, adjoining the palace on the Upper Garden side. At the present time their place is taken by the White (Concert) Hall,

The second room of the Spare Apartment

Rotating-dial clock. Russia. 1780s

Mantel clock. Workshop
of Felix Chopin. 1850s

The third room of the Spare Apartment

while the state rooms continue in the southern enfilade. Its first four rooms had no fixed purpose and were known historically as the Spare Apartment.

In each room the walls are lined with silk with its own pattern, which is typical for the décor of the Great Palace. On display here are authentic works of painting and decorative and applied art from the 18th and 19th centuries: furniture, porcelain, artistic bronze. Particularly noteworthy are portraits of Nicholas I and his daughters by the famous English portraitist George Dawe and the Scottish artist Christina Robertson.

The fourth room of the Spare Apartment

Vase. Imperial
Porcelain Factory,
Russia. 1790s

Table with
a marble top.
France. 1790s

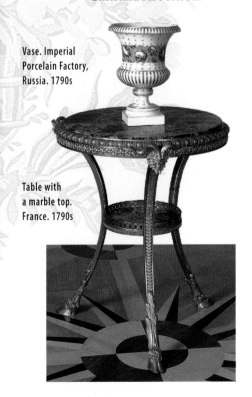

The Crown Room

THE CROWN ROOM, like the Divan Room on the north side to which it is connected by doors, was created in the mid-18th century to Rastrelli's design, then reworked in the 1770s by Yury Veldten. The two rooms are practically a matching pair: here too there is a partition with an alcove, and the walls are lined with painted Chinese silk (in this case depicting the process of making porcelain at the imperial factories of Jingdezhen). Originally this room was known as the Bedchamber. It became the Crown Room during the reign of Paul I when a stand for the imperial crown was installed here.

Gueridon table with a mosaic top. Italy. 18th century

Portable desk. South Germany.
18th century

The Oak Study of Peter the Great

THE STUDY has retained almost completely the appearance given to it in Peter I's time by Le Blond. It was the French architect who suggested using wooden panels with figurative carving, executed by Nicolas Pineau, to decorate the room. The items in the study include Peter I's personal travelling alarm-clock, made by the German craftsman Johannes Benner. Glass panels on its sides allow you to see the mechanism working. On the flap of the desk is a book of *Peter the Great's Decrees from 1714 to 28 January 1725*, published in 1739.

The Oak Staircase

UNTIL RASTRELLI'S reconstruction of the palace the main staircase in the Upper Chambers was the Oak Staircase, situated in the centre of the building. The staircase was created to Jean-Baptiste Alexandre Le Blond's design in 1722–26. The French sculptor Nicolas Pineau was involved in the decoration work, designing the carved handrail. The ceiling painting depicts Aurora, the goddess of the dawn, and is the work of the Russian artist Ivan Vishniakov.

The vault of the
refectory adjoining
the palace church in
the Church Pavilion

Panel: *Christ Walking on the
Water.* Craftsmen under
the direction of Ivan
Vishniakov.
1740s

The Church Pavilion

The Church Pavilion

THE HISTORY of the Church of the Holy Apostles Peter and Paul in the Church Pavilion of the Great Palace began in the year 1747, when Empress Elizabeth embarked on the reconstruction of her father's palace. In the course of four years the Church Pavilion acquired an appearance designed by Francesco Bartolomeo Rastrelli: the three-storey block with a square ground plan was topped by an octagonal dome surmounted by a central gilded cupola and four smaller ones at the corners.

Rastrelli decorated the church interior with especial splendour: abundant gilding, woodcarving and a wealth of colourful painting produced an elevated, festive mood in everyone who entered. All the icons were executed in oil on canvas by a team of painters led by Ivan Vishniakov.

For the next century and a half the church served as the festive setting for marriages and baptisms of members of the House of Romanov and the celebration of religious holidays attended by exalted guests.

The iconostasis of the palace church

38

The Crimson Drawing-Room

The Coat-of-Arms Pavilion

The Special Treasury
in the Coat-of-Arms Pavilion

FRANCESCO Bartolomeo Rastrelli had constructed and decorated this pavilion by the early 1750s. The rich expressiveness of its lines, its exquisite proportions, the sculptural quality of the masses and the clarity of the volumes place it among the most striking achievements in European architecture in the mid-18th century. The pavilion gets its name from the weathervane that crowns it, which was made by Girardon in the form of a heraldic eagle from a model and drawing by Rastrelli. The eagle was given three heads, but from any viewpoint it seems to have two. The gilded decorative carving on the dome and

Miniature portrait of Peter I in a frame.
Artist: Charles Boit. 1717

Fan. France. 1770

Presentation snuffbox commemorating the Russian victory at Kunersdorf during the Seven Years' War. England. 1759

Chandelier.
Poland.
19th century

Bedroom

Study

Today the pavilion's eight rooms – including the state rooms of the northern enfilade – house Peterhof's Special Treasury, a number of memorial items that belonged to Russian rulers from Peter I to Nicholas II, and also a collection of paintings, unique court costumes, furniture and pieces of jewellery.

Dressing Room

the cupola above it was executed under the guidance of the master craftsman Josef Stahlmeyer in 1751. The rooms inside the building were finished to designs by Rastrelli (with the participation of Stahlmeyer, Bernhard Egg, A. Voronin and others). Under Catherine II they were partially refurbished by Veldten.

The Great Cascade

THE GREAT Cascade is Peterhof's chief adornment – a grand, magnificently decorated monument to Russia's victories in the Northern War, a unique artistic ensemble of world significance. With its scale, incorporating over 70 fountains, its wealth of sculptural decoration and, last not least, the astonishing unity and expressiveness of all the elements in the ensemble, it occupies one of the leading places among the world's fountain installations.

Surviving rough sketches made by Peter I himself are evidence that he was the person who came up with the idea of a cascade below the Upper Chambers. Its construction began no later than 1715, when, on 24 January, Peter issued a decree specifying work for the coming summer. The architects Braunstein, Le Blond, Michetti and Zemtsov were involved in the project, as well as the fountain specialist Paul Sualem. At its grand formal inauguration on 13 August 1723 the splendour of the cascade amazed everyone.

THE ARCHITECTURAL basis of the cascade is a grand spreading "staircase" (with an area of about 300 square metres) descending down the terrace from the platform of the Upper (Small) Grotto. Around 60 fountains were placed on the steps and platforms. The water they discharge pours first into the Scoop basin and then flows along the 500-metre-long, 12-metre-wide Sea Canal into the Gulf of Finland. The Scoop was probably begun as early as 1715. It was originally rectangular, but in 1716 Le Blond turned it into a semicircle.

In Peter's time the canal, the axis of the Lower Park, dug out in 1715–16, was navigable. The movement of vessels along it was aided by locks constructed by the engineer Vasily Tuvolkov in 1723. With the installation of

the *Samson* fountain in the centre of the Scoop, vessels no longer ran up the canal to the palace. Only on festive occasions did yachts enter the canal, when it became part of the colourful illuminations. The canal is adorned by an alley of 22 fountains spurting from marble bowls and 22 mask fountains in the form of lions' heads attached to it granite-clad walls. The banks of the canal are connected by two bridges – the Maliban (after 1740) and Marly (1723, reconstructed in the late 1700s). The latter provides a striking view of the Great Palace from the Gulf of Finland.

The *Trumpeting Tritons* fountain

The central hall of the Lower Grotto

The Sculpture of the Great Cascade

THE SCUPTURAL decoration of the cascade included some 250 pieces made of bronze, lead and marble, over 30 of which are also fountains. This ensemble of plastic art extolling Russia's naval triumph was almost a century in the making. It was begun back in Peter I's time when, according to the documents, as early as February 1717 gilded lead statues – 60 large and 20 small – were delivered to Peterhof from Amsterdam. In 1721–22 metal castings for the reliefs, masks, figured brackets and more arrived from England. Another consignment of sculpture

was delivered from The Hague in 1723. Originally the pieces were made to drawings and models by Le Blond, Braunstein, Konrad Ossner, C.B. Rastrelli, Niccolo Michetti and François Vassou. The cascade was made particularly striking by the decoration of the walls of its ledges with figured brackets and gilded bas-reliefs on a rich blue-green background. In 1735 the sculptural ensemble was augmented by the famous *Samson* and three years later by the *Trumpeting Tritons*.

By the end of the 18th century the lead statues had become deformed under the influence of the water and it was decided to replace them in bronze. By 1806, 32 new statues had been produced – some were copies of ancient masterpieces, others original, designed by such eminent sculptors as Ivan Prokofiev (*Tritons, The Volkhov and Acis*), Feodosy Shchedrin (*Perseus, The Neva and Sirens*), Ivan Martos (*Actaeon*), Fedot Shubin (*Pandora*) and Jacques Dominique Rachette (*Galatea, Jupiter, Juno and Naiads and Tritons*).

Statue of *Jupiter*. From a model by Jacques Dominique Rachette. 1801

Statute of the *Callipygian* Venus. After an ancient original. 1800

Statue of *Perseus*. After a model by Feodosy Shchedrin. 1801

Statue of *Actaeon*. After a model by Ivan Martos. 1801

The Grottoes of the Great Cascade

THE FAMOUS grottoes (a word of Italian origin for a small natural or artificial cavern) – Lower and Upper, or Large and Small – give the Great Cascade a special mysterious attraction. The Large Grotto, construction of which began in the spring of 1715, is the heart of the cascade. Its 9-metre is pierced by five archways leading to its tufa-lined interior. The extensive platform in front of the grotto contains the *Basket* fountain (originally the *Wheel*). Twenty-eight inclined jets spurt from its outer ring of tufa, creating an elegant frame for the tall jets of

the central ring. The design of the fountain was devised by Peter I, while the idea evidently came from Le Blond, who included "playing water" as well as "falling water" in his new project for the Great Cascade. In 1858–60 Nikolai Benois made the pattern of the *Wheel*'s small jets more elaborate, after which it became known as the *Basket*. The interior of the Large Grotto is adorned with marble busts and gilded statues. In 1728–29, after Peter I's death, but to his design, a "stone table with splashing" trick fountain was installed.

The *Borghese Warrior* fountain. After an ancient original of the 1st century AD

The *Sirens* fountain. After a model by Feodosy Shchedrin. 1805

The *Volkhov* fountain by the Great Scoop. From a model by Ivan Prokofiev. 1805

THE SMALL (Upper) Grotto, whose low (about 3 metre) but extensive (the full 42-metre width of the Great Cascade) wall is broken up by recessed panels and arched niches, was created after Peter expressed the wish in 1721 to have "two small grottoes" above the Large Grotto. The task was solved by Michetti, who embellished the wall of the new grotto with mask-fountains of *Bacchus* and *Neptune*, placed the gilded bas-reliefs already mentioned on the risers of the cascade steps and also added two balustrades to the ensemble – on the edge of the platform of the Small Grotto and on the edge of the terrace by the palace. In 1724 Peter I gave orders for Carlo Bartolomeo Rastrelli to make larger masks for the *Bacchus* and *Neptune* fountains, which became 2 metres tall. These fountains are the symbolic sources of the Great Cascade. In 1738 Michetti installed Rastrelli's *Trumpeting Tritons* in line with the marble balustrade on the platform of the Upper Grotto.

The *Samson* fountain

The Scoop Basin and the *Samson* fountain

ALL THE WATER that flows in the Great Cascade, its greater and lesser fountains, pours down the marble steps and ultimately flows into a large, almost semicircular basin. But even there it does not find peace, becoming caught up in the watery symphony of this Scoop, around whose shores pagan deities send forth ever more streams of water.

In 1735 the Scoop was adorned by the *Samson* fountain – the unarguable apotheosis of Peterhof's watery magnificence, created for the celebration of the 25th anniversary of Battle of Poltava in 1709. The subject of the 3.3-metre sculpture symbolizing Russia's victory over Sweden was inspired by a series of associations. The great battle took place on 27 June, the feast of the obscure 6th-century Orthodox saint Sampsonius. His name in turn evoked the biblical hero Samson who famously wrestled with a lion, the beast that appears in the Swedish coat-of-arms.

The original sculptural group was cast in lead from a model by Carlo Bartolomeo Rastrelli. In 1801 it was replaced with a bronze version sculpted by Mikhail Kozlovsky. Samson is the tallest fountain in Peterhof, soaring to a height of 19–20 metres.

The Lower Park

THE FORMAL Lower Park is Peterhof's best-known component, the one that brought it world fame. This unique work of garden and park design laid out with precise symmetry was created over a prolonged period. Its appearance changed over time and today it is a reflection of various historical eras. The park occupies an elongated rectangle with an area of over 100 hectares. It extends along the shore of the Gulf of Finland for 2.5 kilometres, while its width north to south is just 500 metres. The three ensembles – central,

western and eastern – within the Lower Park neatly complement one other. The composition of the park is based on avenues radiating from several points and intersecting each other. The main ones lead to the sea or end in a fountain. The central feature of the park is the Sea Canal. Equidistant from it are Peterhof's famous *Adam* and *Eve* fountains, the *Chessboard Hill* and *Golden Hill* cascades, the Monplaisir complex and the Hermitage pavilion.

The Great Parterres

The Great Parterres

EXTENDING over the open area at the foot of the Great Cascade are the Great Parterres, perhaps the most attractive compositions in the Lower Park. In the 18th century ensembles of lawns, flowerbeds, ponds and hedges were arranged in geometrical patterns always following the Baroque principle of mirror symmetry. Areas laid out in this way were inspired by French proto-

The *Nymph* fountain

The *Danaid* fountain

A terrace fountain

types and known in Russia and elsewhere as French gardens. The Great Parterres at Peterhof were created by the master gardener Bernhard Fock. In line with *Samson* on either side are fountain bowls with 10-metre jets: the western Italian (the Italian Baratini brothers took charge of its construction) and the eastern French (created by the French specialist Paul Sualem).

On the slope of the terrace descending to the Great Parterres are ten small cascades with water flowing in steps to stone bowls above which thin jets of water rise. The compositions, known as the Terrace Fountains, were created in 1799–1801 by the architect Franz Brouer and fountain engineer Feodor Strelnikov to a design by Andrei Voronikhin. Originally the steps were made of Pudost limestone, but in the 1850s Andrei Stakenschneider replaced them with marble.

Sculpture of a lion by one of the Voronikhin Colonnades

The Voronikhin Colonnades

ON THE NORTH side the parterres are bounded by two finely proportioned colonnades with gilded domes and vases. Their 21-metre long facades separate the flower beds from the woodland area of the park. The granite steps of the colonnades flanked by figures of reclining lions lead into galleries that are adorned by eight paired Doric columns made of grey Serdobol granite. The outer walls of the colonnades are faced with marble and pierced by large window openings. Erected to replace dilapidated wooden structures in 1800–03 to the design of Andrei Voronikhin, the colonnades are named after him. On the roof of each of them are three decorative vase-fountains spurting water.

The Orangery block

The *Triton* fountain

The Orangery Garden

TO THE EAST of the Great Parterres lies the small Orangery Garden, a traditional ensemble from Peter's time. The history of this area goes back to 1722, when Peter I gave orders "to build an orangery". The design was probably the work of the architect Michetti, while construction, in 1722–25, was overseen by Johann Friedrich Braunstein. While creating a service building where plants in tubs, bulbs and tubers were kept in winter, the architects gave it the look of a smart palatial pavilion with a rounded façade.

The Orangery Garden is adorned by a fountain with the sculptural group of *A Triton Tearing Apart the Jaws of a Sea-Monster* created in 1726 from models by Bartolomeo Carlo Rastrelli. Contemporaries would have readily understood its allegorical meaning: the Triton stood for the young Russian navy inflicting a crushing defeat on a Swedish squadron at the Battle of Gangut on 27 July 1714.

The Roman Fountains

THE ROMAN FOUNTAIN parterre in the eastern part of the Lower Park was laid out in the mid-1700s by the gardener Bernhard Fock. He created sunken "bowling-green" lawns planted with annual and perennial flowers. The idea for the paired fountains each with five jets goes back to Peter's time, but they appeared in the park only in 1739 to the design of Johann Blank and Ivan Davydov, assisted by the fountain engineer

Paul Sualem. In 1756 Francesco Bartolomeo Rastrelli changed the appearance of the fountains by replacing the bowls with discs. In 1800 the wooden fountains were rebuilt in granite and marble. Later they were embellished with bronze masks cast from models by the sculptor Ivan Martos. Inspired by the fountains on the square in front of St Peter's Basilica in Rome, the pair became known as the Roman Fountains.

The Chessboard Hill Cascade

POWERFUL STREAMS of water pour from the jaws of dragons guarding the entrance to the upper grotto of the *Dragon Hill* cascade. This elaborate construction is flanked by personages from ancient mythology: Neptune, Jupiter, Andromeda, Flora, Pomona, Ceres, Vulcan and Pluto – marble statues made by Italian sculptors in the early 1700s. The concept for this feature belonged to Peter the Great, whose specification of it was inspired by one he saw at the French royal residence of Marly. The Tsar wanted to have "a marble cascade with

a small grotto and a wild hill". The architects Braunstein, Michetti, Zemtsov and Usov were all involved in its long genesis, completing the work in 1739. The main finishing materials were tufa and oyster shells. In 1769 the wooden steps of the cascade were replaced and painted checkerboard-fashion, after which it was also known as the Chessboard Hill. In the 19th century the cascade was repeatedly reconstructed, but during the post-war reconstruction the restorers gave it back its 18th-century appearance.

The Monument to Peter the Great

ON 8 MAY 1884, the 200th anniversary of the birth of the founder of Peterhof, a monument to Peter the Great sculpted by Mark Antokolsky was set up at the intersection of the Monplaisir and Marly Avenues.

The Pyramid Fountain

THE PYRAMID is one of the most original pieces of fountain design and uses the most water of any installation in the Lower Park. In 1721, on Peter I's orders, Niccolo Michetti produced a design for a reproduction of the *Obelisk* fountain at Versailles. But the Tsar decided to change the shape of the figure, making it

four-sided instead of three. The work was begun in 1721 under the direction of the architect Mikhail Zemtsov and the fountain engineer Paul Sualem (a relative of Rennequin Sualem, the creator of the celebrated "Marly machine") and completed shortly before Peter's death. The Holsteiner Bergholtz wrote: "There is not another such large and beautiful water jet perhaps anywhere." The maximum water consumption was over 150 litres every second forming an eight-metre four-sided seven-stepped pyramid. The effect was achieved by reducing the diameters of the 505 copper nozzles towards the centre of the fountain. As the water pressure rose, so did the height of the jets, and the glistening foaming mass of water, framed by a marble balustrade with vases, resembled a pyramid. This watery obelisk was an unusual monument to the conclusion of the Northern War in 1721.

The Sun Fountain

FROM THE MONUMENT to Peter I the Monplaisir Alley runs north to that Tsar's favourite palace – Monplaisir. On the way is another ensemble from the founder's era – the Menagerie Garden that was created in 1719 by the architects Le Blond and Braunstein for the menagerie that Peter planned. The main sight of this garden is the *Sun* fountain that has a history going back to 1721 when the Tsar gave orders to "make a fountain in the pond where the menagerie is." In June 1723 the fountain designed by Michetti was completed and tested

with water. Peter had it modified several times. In 1775 to the design of the architect Yury Veldten (assisted by Ivan Yakovlev) the fountain was remade in the form of a rotating column attached to the top of which was a round construction with 187 openings. The jets of water emerging from them resembled the rays of the sun and so the fountain acquired its present name. Today it is a very rare surviving example of an 18th-century mechanical fountain.

The Eastern Aviary and Swan Pond

Painting inside the dome of the Eastern Aviary. 1722

The Aviaries

THE AVIARIES – two elegant wooden structures – were built following a French fashion of the 16th and 17th centuries, when "poultry yards" and dovecotes could be found everywhere. Their design has been attributed to the architect Michetti. Inside they are decorated with exquisite painting with gold highlights, believed to be by Louis Caravaque. In the 18th century cages containing songbirds were placed in the aviaries each summer: nightingales, thrushes, longspurs, siskins, chaffinches, redpolls, bullfinches, exotic parrots, canaries and others. For peafowl and pheasants large wire enclosures were set up. The birds were moved for the winter to the Poultry Farm located to the west of the Marly area.

The Trick Fountains

ONE OF THE GREATEST attractions of Peterhof is the famous trick fountains, the fashion for which Peter the Great, who had a great fondness for jokes and curiosities, brought back from abroad where such amusements were exceptionally popular at the court of Louis XIV.

One of the oldest practical jokes of this sort – the "Water Road" – was created by Michetti on the Monplaisir Alley at Peter's prompting. The essence of the joke was that the path suddenly became covered with an arch of water, splashing the strollers. Guests first got to experience this effect in 1721. The amusement was a hit and invariably raised the mood. Another of the trick fountains – the *Umbrella* – was constructed in 1796 to the design of the architect Franz Brouer. The fountain's hidden jets form a solid

curtain barring the way out from beneath the canopy of the umbrella. The *Little Oak* fountain produced to Carlo Bartolomeo Rastrelli's design in 1735 originally stood in the Upper Garden. The fountain engineer Feodor Strelnikov turned it in a "natural tree" with green leaves surrounded by "tulips", while placing two wooden benches with nozzles hidden in their backs close by. Visitors who sat down to rest would be unexpectedly squirted, causing peals of laughter. The nearby *Little Firs*, installed in 1784, took the form of little metal conifers painted natural colours, but if anyone approached, fine sprays of water squirted from their branches.

The *Little Firs*, *Little Oak*, *Bench* and *Umbrella* fountains

The *Sheaf* fountain and the *Faun* cloche fountain in the Monplaisir Garden

The Monplaisir Ensemble

THE MONPLAISIR palace, the chief structure in the seashore ensemble, fully reflects the character of Peterhof's great founder and the spirit of his age. The name "Monplaisir" means "my delight" in French. In Europe the term was traditionally used for places out in the country, underlining their private purpose. The Tsar dreamt of a house by the sea and personally chose its site. The central part of the palace, covered with a mansard roof with a carved vase in the centre, stood on a small headland. Peter himself sketched the intended layout of the

building that was begun in May 1714. He sought to have his new home conform to the concepts of comfort and convenience that he had acquired during his time in Holland. The decoration of the interior resembled that in the suburban residences of the rich burghers of Amsterdam. Those who worked on the Monplaisir ensemble included the architects Schlüter, Braunstein, Le Blond and Michetti and the decorative artists Nicolas Pineau, Philippe Pillement, Louis Caravaque and Jean Michel. The palace became the Tsar's maritime residence, a sort of celebration of Russia's victory in the struggle for access to the sea.

The Monplaisir Palace

"PRESSING my eyes to the old windows that went down to the ground, I dimly made out what was inside through the thick, slightly uneven panes: a black-and-white checkerboard floor and some long corridors with painted ceilings and paintings hung on their dark oak walls. I particularly liked an enchanting little room covered all over with white and blue vases on gilded consoles. If I peered for long into that enchanted world, then it would seem that the door was about to open and the enormous Tsar would come come striding in from another room and cast me a stern glance," Alexander Benois wrote of Monplaisir.

The Lacquer Cabinet

The Maritime Cabinet

The Central Hall

The Gallery

By the early 18th century the Orient was in fashion and *chinoiserie* ornament was extensively used. The Lacquer Cabinet at Monplaisir, designed by Johann Friedrich Braunstein, was one of the first interiors in Russia in the Chinese style. Its 94 lacquer panels painted with multi-figure compositions were created by a ten-man team of talented Russian icon-painters under the guidance of Hendrik van Brunkhorst.

To embellish his palace Peter followed his fascination with the sea and shipbuilding, giving preference to sea-scapes. He had built up a collection of Western European paintings and used it to adorn his beloved palace. The Monplaisir collection numbered 201 works and 120 canvases have survived to this day. At Monplaisir, in the fresh air on the seashore, Peter felt like a captain on the deck of a ship and from here he could sail across to the warships anchored in the distant Kronstadt roads.

The Catherine Block

THIS BLOCK was constructed by Francesco Bartolomeo Rastrelli in place of the old Monplaisir orangery. After the building was completed in 1748, work continued for another ten years and more on the interior decoration. The rooms were finished with Rastrelli's usual gilded woodcarving, fabric wallpaper and patterned parquet floors. Under Empress Elizabeth the building was used for small balls, concerts, masquerades and card games. When Peter III came to the throne, a wooden wing of the building became his wife Catherine's summer residence. It was from here on 28 June 1762 that she went off to St Petersburg, where with the aid of the Guards she seized power and was proclaimed ruling empress.

Alexander I's Bedroom

The Yellow Hall

The Blue Drawing-Room

In 1785–86 on Catherine II's orders the architect Giacomo Quarenghi, assisted by the sculptor Jacques Dominique Rachette and the decorative artist Carlo Scotti, refurbished eight rooms of the block in the Neo-Classical style, using pilasters, stuccowork and grisaille painting that imitates mouldings. In 1810 rooms in the palace were decorated in the Empire style but following that no further changes were made. The ornate, elegant interiors are complemented by furniture from the late 18th and early 19th centuries made to designs by Carlo Rossi, Andrei Voronikhin and Vasily Stasov specially for Peterhof. The grandest room, the Yellow Hall, is used to display the celebrated Guryev Service that was commissioned from the Imperial Porcelain Factory in 1809, when its director was Count Dmitry Guryev. Work on the service continued until the late 19th century and with 5,000 items it is one of Russia's largest ensembles of porcelain.

The Bathhouse Block

The Bath and Kitchen Blocks

The Cold Bath

THE BATH AND KITCHEN Blocks at Monplaisir provide fascinating insights into Russian daily life in the 18th and 19th centuries. The service buildings, the western and eastern galleries, were built onto Monplaisir in 1719–21 to Braunstein's design to accommodate guests. Mikhail Zemtsov built a Bathhouse next to the eastern gallery and in 1726 work began on the Kitchen block to the south of it. In Elizabeth's time Rastrelli constructed a new bathhouse with a bathing pool and fountain. Under Catherine II the pool was reconstructed to draw seawater from the Gulf. Paul I had Quarenghi replace the wooden Bathhouse with a masonry one. In the 19th century a bathhouse for the ladies and gentlemen of the court was constructed here.

The Monplaisir Bathhouse was used by Emperor Nicholas I's family. Empress Alexandra Feodorovna took therapeutic baths in a wooden wing. In 1866, in place of Rastrelli's wing Eduard Hahn constructed a masonry Bath Block that was fitted out for the hydrotherapy used to treat Empress Maria Alexandrovna, the wife of Alexander II, for consumption.

The room with the «great shower» in the bathhouse for gentlemen of the court

The Assembly Hall is situated beyond the Bath Block, under the same roof as the Pantry, Kitchen and Coffee Pantry. All these places date back to 1725, when Catherine I gave orders for construction by Monplaisir of "kitchen chambers and other rooms in accordance with the drawing made by the architect Zemtsov". The

The Assembly Hall

The *America* tapestry.
1730s-50s

oak-panelled walls of the Assembly Hall are decorated with 17 tapestries woven in the first half of the 18th century at the St Petersburg Tapestry Factory. Tapestry was also used to upholster the Russian-made chairs from the 1720s. The Kitchen, made to Rastrelli's design in the mid-1700s, contains a variety of old utensils and tableware. Exquisite dishes for the imperial court were produced here by a succession of famous chefs who are also part of Peterhof's history: Veldten under Peter I, Fuchs under Elizabeth, Carême under Alexander I, Cubat under Alexander II, and others. The Coffee Pantry next to the Kitchen was a tribute to the fashion for the drink introduced by Peter I.

The Kitchen

The Adam and Eve Fountains

FROM MONPLAISIR two paths leading south-west bring visitors to the Marly Avenue – to the spot occupied by the *Adam* fountain, one of the oldest in Peterhof. The fountain is a companion piece to *Eve*, which also stands on the Marly Avenue, in the western part of the Lower Park. Installation of these two fountains began in 1720 and they were intended to symbolize the marriage between Peter I and Catherine I. Their locations at the junctions of avenues in the eastern and western parts of the park, equidistant from the Sea Canal, make them nodal points in the composition of the park. The marble sculptures of Adam and Eve were made in Venice to a commission from Peter I by the sculptor Giovanni Bonazza in 1717. They are free copies of famous works by Antonio Rizzi that adorn the Palace of the Doges. The pair were set in the centre of identical 17-metre-diameter octagonal basins. From the base of each of the pedestals sixteen jets spurt to a height of 6½ metres, forming a crown-like decoration of water. *Adam* was put into operation first, during Peter's lifetime. The *Eve* fountain, created by Timofei Usov to the same design on the orders of Catherine I, was inaugurated in 1726.

The lift mechanism of the table

The Hermitage Pavilion

IN A PART of the Lower Park remote from the Great Palace you will find the exceptionally attractive Hermitage pavilion. It is surrounded by a deep water-filled moat crossed by a bridge that in the 18th century was a drawbridge. The first Hermitage (a place to withdraw and enjoy seclusion) in Russia that became a prototype for many similar buildings was constructed to the design of Johann Friederich Braunstein in 1721–25. Following his passion for seafaring Peter ordered that the facades of the pavilion be decorated with copies of the railing on his flagship *Ingermanlandia* from which in 1716 he had commanded the combined fleets of Russia, Britain, Holland and Denmark. The great curiosity of the Hermitage was a large oval table for 14 diners with a central section that could be lowered to the floor below, laid with dishes and drinks and sent back up to the Pavilion Hall so that meals could be taken in private. In this same hall the celebrated Russian dramatist Denis Fonvizin read his comedy *The Brigadier* in the presence of Catherine II. In 1759 the walls of the hall were decorated with 17th- and 18th-century Flemish, Dutch, French, Italian and German paintings to a plan devised by Rastrelli.

The Pavilion Hall

The Battle of Poltava. Copy by an unknown 18th-century artist of the painting by Ivan Nikitin. 1727

The Apostle Paul. Artist: Georg Gsell. 1700–40

The Lion Cascade

NICCOLO MICHETTI produced drawings for a fountain to be installed at the end of an avenue leading from the Hermitage Pavilion, but the architect's concept was never realized. The composition that was created at the end of the 18th century to the design of Andrei Voronikhin consisted of eight fountain vases on a stone base and the paired figures, traditional for that time, of Hercules and Flora that were replaced just a year later by bronze statues of lions that gave the cascade its name. In the middle of the 19th century a new cascade was constructed to the design of Andrei Stakenschneider. It took the form of a massive colonnade of

fourteen 8-metre-tall Ionic columns carved from grey Serdobol granite that is widely used in St Petersburg architecture. The capitals of the columns and the shallow fountain bowls were made from white Italian Carrara marble. The craftsmen of the Peterhof Lapidary Works were involved in creating them. Placed in the centre of the cascade is a statue of Aganippe, the nymph of a spring at the foot of Mount Helicon, where the muses were said to gather. Streams of water flowed from the nymph's jug and the jaws of the lions standing at the sides of the colonnade.

The Whale Fountain

CLOSE TO the cascade is the *Whale* fountain in the Sandy Pond. Its name comes from an 18th-century sculptural group. Later the dilapidated statues were removed and what we see today is a composition created in the 19th century by the fountain engineer Feodor Strelnikov. South of the Lion Cascade is a marble bench dedicated to the memory of Grand Duchess Alexandra Nikolayevna that once stood in Alexandria. Nicholas I's youngest daughter's death in childbirth in 1844 was an irreparable loss for the imperial family. The bench, faced with different varieties of marble and decorated with a bust of Alexandra Nikolayevna sculpted by Ivan Vitali, served the Emperor as a place for melancholy reflection.

The *Nymph Aganippe* fountain of the Lion Cascade

The Memorial Bench

The *Whale* fountain

The Marly Ensemble

LOCATED in the western part of the Lower Park, the Marly palace ensemble received its name in memory of Peter the Great's visit to Marly-le-Roi, the French royal residence outside Paris. In 1717, from early May to the second half of June, the Russian Tsar acquainted himself with the environs of Versailles and what he saw made an indelible impression on him. At Peterhof, though, the Tsar did not seek to copy the French prototype: in creating the palace his architects were guided by his tastes and directions.

On the east side of the palace is the Marly Pond. On the west the building is adjoined by an almost semi-circular pond, divided into sections. This played more than a decorative role. At Peterhof fish brought from remote parts of Russia were bred for the Tsar's table. Not long before Peter's death they began to keep sturgeon here and today the tradition of angling in the Sectoral Pond has been revived.

The Vestibule

Long-case clock. Made
by W. Koster. First third
of the 18th century

The Marly Palace

REFINED modesty is the hallmark of this palace that was built
in 1720–25 to the design of Johann Friedrich Braunstein. The small
building contains just sixteen rooms, a staircase and two corridors. In
the original concept it was to be a single-storey building, but when
roofing began, Peter gave orders for a second floor to be added as it

The Kitchen

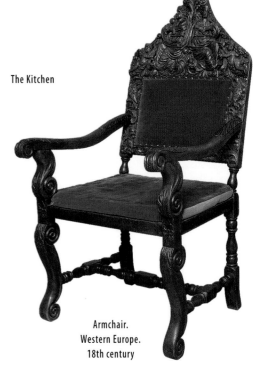

Armchair.
Western Europe.
18th century

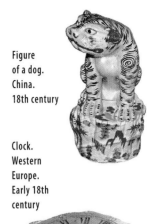

Figure
of a dog.
China.
18th century

Clock.
Western
Europe.
Early 18th
century

The Bedroom

The Oak Study

became clear that it was out of proportion with the size of the excavated pond. The decoration of the facades is extremely simple – only the balconies stand out with their sculpted brackets and wrought-iron railings where gold scrolls glitter among the black curves.

Inside the Marly Palace is simple and comfortable. The building lacks the traditional grand hall: Peter allotted that role to the Vestibule. The Dining-Room, the Oak and Plane-Tree Studies, decorated with panels with add-on carving, and the Bedroom, lined with a floral-pattern fabric, are not only cosy, but also elegant. The palace's small staircase is decorated with an open-work rocaille railing whose elaborate pattern incorporates relief images of single-headed eagles and crowns.

The display includes furniture from Peter's time, books from the imperial library, a table with a schist top made by the Tsar himself and tableware that belonged to him. The palace's collection of paintings is typical for Peter's time, comprising 17th- and 18th-century Dutch, Flemish and Italian works by Abraham Storck, Pietro Belotti, Andrea Celesti and others.

The Golden Hill Cascade

THE EXCEPTIONALLY ornate regular layout of the Marly ensemble, the most attractive in this part of the park, was achieved by creating three areas arranged symmetrically around the palace. A large smooth pond was dug out in front of the east façade of the palace, accentuating the elegance of the building. To the south of the palace is a parterre with fountains; to the north the "Garden of Venus". The soil excavated to make the pond was used to construct the Marly Bank – a 3-metre-high rampart around 250 metres long, later reinforced by a brick wall.

At the centre of the embankment that prevents the Baltic winds from entering the garden area a balustraded platform was constructed. It provides a striking view of the sea with Kronstadt and St Petersburg clearly visible. Below the embankment a formal garden was laid out with three round areas, on the central one of which a marble sculpture of the *Venus Medici* (a 19th-century copy of the ancient original) was installed.

View of the Marly area from the *Golden Hill* cascade

The statue of the *Venus Medici* in the Garden of Venus.
After an ancient original. Between 1830 and 1860

IN 1721 Peter ordered the construction in the western part of the Lower Park of a cascade like the one he had seen at Marly-le-Roi. This was called the Marly Cascade and later the name was extended to the entire ensemble. The cascade was designed by Michetti in collaboration with Carlo Bartolomeo Rastrelli. Later responsibility for the project passed to Mikhail Zemtsov, who completed it in 1732. The steps of the cascade were faced with sheets of gilded copper, which gave the second name – "Golden Hill".

At the foot of the cascade a shallow basin was constructed with a marble statue of a *Faun with a Kid* in the centre. The wall at the top was adorned by sculptures of Neptune, a triton and a nymph, while *Andromeda* and *Flora* in marble with dolphins spouting water were placed by the bottom step. The sculptural decoration was supplemented by wooden figures, later replaced by lead ones. In 1870 the cascade was refurbished under the direction of the architect Nikolai Benois: its steps were faced with marble, while the dilapidated figures were replaced with marble statues "of mythological content" brought from Italy that had been created by unknown 19th-century craftsmen after ancient originals.

The *Ménager* fountains

TO THE WEST of the Marly ensemble there is a monument of *Peter I with the Young Louis XV in His Arms* that was cast in 1899 from a model by the sculptor Leopold Bernstamm. The subject was inspired by an episode during Peter's visit to France in 1717: the Tsar took the boy King in his arms and exclaimed, "I am carrying the whole of France by myself!" After this encounter in the Tuileries the Tsar wrote to his wife: "The child is most handsome in looks and figure and quite wise for his age, which is seven years." This monument to Peter I was lost during the war. In 2005 the composition, recreated by the sculptor Nikolai Karlykhanov, was reinstated on its historical site.

Statue of *Peter I with the Young Louis XV in His Arms.* After a model by Leopold Bernstamm. 1899

The Alexandria Park

ALEXANDRIA – an extensive (115-hectare) landscape park to the east of the Lower Park – is an outstanding example of 19th-century park design. The main work of creating it was carried out in 1826–29 by the master gardener Peter Ehrler working to a project drawn up by the architect Adam Menelaws. Features of the natural relief were successfully used in the park. The low-lying shore of the Gulf of Finland forms a coastal terrace that ends in a steep slope rising to an upper terrace. The difference in height is 8–12 metres, which made it possible to create some very effective vistas at Alexandria.

The Hops Veranda. Architect: Eduard Hahn. 1849

The central building of the park is the Cottage palace, constructed in 1826–29 to Adam Menelaws's design. It was begun straight after Nicholas I's instruction dating from spring 1826 for the construction here of "a country house or so-called 'cotich' with all utilities in combination with a park". The Emperor presented the estate to his wife, Alexandra Feodorovna, in whose honour it was named.

In time the Alexandria ensemble came to include a number of splendid edifices, most notably the Farm Palace and the Church of Alexander Nevsky (the Gothic Chapel). They are comple-

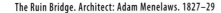

The Ruin Bridge. Architect: Adam Menelaws. 1827–29

The *Gothic Well* summerhouse.
Architect: A. Charlemagne. 1835

mented by less grand, but very striking structures – the Ruin Bridge across the Shchegolev stream on the road linking the Cottage and the Gothic Chapel, the Gothic Well and others.

The Cottage Palace

THE DÉCOR and furnishings of the palace organically combine refined splendour with domestic comfort. There are no grand state rooms traditional for an imperial palace: Nicholas provided for his family life in fairly small apartments where every element in the decoration was rational and planned. On the ground floor of the Cottage were Alexandra Feodorovna's rooms and those for general use; on the floor above the rooms of Nicholas I and the children, and at the top rooms for the courtiers in attendance. The central feature of the building was a fine cast-iron staircase made at the Alexandrovsky Foundry in St Petersburg.

The décor incorporated the arms of Alexandria designed by the poet Vasily Zhukovsky: a sword passing through a wreath of white roses on a blue ground and the motto *For Faith, Tsar and Country*. Gothic motifs – lancet arches, spires and turrets – occurred everywhere in the decoration of rooms and objects. With touching tenderness the mistress of the palace filled its rooms with keepsakes connected with the memory of her parents, King Frederick William III of Prussia and Queen Louise.

The Main Staircase

The Drawing-Room

Empress Alexandra Feodorovna was the heart and soul of her large family. This charming delicate woman was very suited by the poetic nickname "the White Rose" that she was given back in childhood in her parents' home at a time of general infatuation with knightly romances. Zhukovsky, who taught the German princess Russian, said: "Her heart is open almost like an infant's; her mind is beautiful." Alexandra Feodorovna was one of the finest looking women of her day. Her marriage to Nicholas I was considered extremely happy. The Empress bore her husband seven children. She was devoid of personal ambition, remote from any desire to wield power, invariably eager only to do good. She was active in public life and known as one of the chief philanthropists of the period.

Grand receptions and banquets were as a rule held in the Great Palace at Peterhof, but the Cottage also had a large Dining-Room, created in an extension that Andrei Stakenschneider added to the building. It contained a table and oak chairs with high carved backs upholstered with crimson cloth bearing the arms of Alexandria. There was a specially made service with which to lay the table and the décor was complemented by a collection of items made of coloured glass (ruby, cobalt and uranium) with Gothic stylization.

Portrait of Empress Alexandra Feodorovna. Sculptor: Christian Daniel Rauch. Late 1820s

Clock in the form of a rose. Western Europe. Second quarter of the 19th century

The Library

The Dining-Room

The last occupants of the Cottage – Nicholas I's grandson, Emperor Alexander III and his wife, Maria Feodorovna – kept the palace as it had been under its first owners with the exception of a few rooms. On the ground floor a Small Reception Room appeared in the Second Rococo style with figurines made at the Meissen factory from 18th-century models.

Upstairs Maria Feodorovna created for herself a Bedroom and Study in the then-popular Moderne (Art Nouveau) style. The Empress's authentic bed now in the Bedroom came from the yacht *Poliarnaya Zvezda* on which Maria Feodorovna paid frequent visits to her Danish homeland. In the Empress's Study the walls are decorated with Karelian birch panels on which there are little shelves for fashionable trinkets. Particularly noteworthy among them is the porcelain produced at the Royal Factory in Copenhagen. The Study is also adorned by vases of etched multi-layered glass created in France by Emile Gallé's firm and that of the Daum brothers. There is also maple furniture made to designs from the architect Mikhail Krasovsky.

Maria Feodorovna Study

Clock. France. 1829

Decorative plate with a portrait of Nicholas I on horseback. The Royal Porcelain Factory, Berlin, Germany. 1830s

Willows and Irises vase. The Royal Porcelain Factory, Copenhagen, Danish. 1895

Item from a dressing-table set with the Alexandria coat-of-arms. Imperial Porcelain Factory, St Petersburg, Russia. Second quarter of the 19th century

Cup and saucer. The Royal Porcelain Factory, Copenhagen, Danish. Early 1900s

The Gothic Chapel

THE GOTHIC CHAPEL or Church of St Alexander Nevsky was the domestic church of the imperial family. With its fine silhouette reminiscent of the mediaeval cathedrals of Germany and France, the Chapel fits organically into the picturesque Alexandria Park, being set off by the romantic landscape. In 1829 Nicholas I commissioned a design for a small Gothic church from

Sculpture: *The Apostle Peter with Keys.*
After a model by Vasily Demuth-Malinovsky

The interior of the Gothic Chapel

the eminent Prussian architect Karl Friedrich Schinkel. The foundation stone was laid on 24 May 1831 in the presence of the entire imperial family and their retinue. Construction was overseen by Adam Menelaws and completed after his death by Joseph Charlemagne. The exterior is adorned by 43 figures chased from copper sheeting following models by the sculptor Vasily Demuth-Malinovsky. The interior still retains an iconostasis with icons by the painter Timofei Neff.

the established tradition at Alexandria he gave the façade a Gothic look. On the east side the building has a utility area with an ice-house and on the south there is a fine garden.

Since 2011 the Palace Telegraph Station museum has functioned in Alexandria, presenting the history of Russian equipment, the importance of long-distance communications in people's lives and the labours of the operators who once lived and worked at the station.

The Imperial Telegraph Station

POSSESSING a natural inclination towards engineering and technology, Nicholas I devoted particular attention to the problems of communications between the centre of his colossal empire and its outlying regions. In 1827 he set up the Telegraph Committee to choose the best optical telegraph system. This provided the vital link between the residence in Peterhof and ministers and heads of the armed forces in Kronstadt, St Petersburg and Warsaw, but due to its dependence on weather conditions a better solution was required.

The next stage of technical progress was the electromagnetic telegraph. As early as the 1850s this new method of communication was in active use between St Petersburg, Peterhof and Kronstadt.

Continuing what his father had begun, Alexander II chose a new site for the station and in 1859 the telegraph moved to a specially constructed building on the boundary between the imperial residence and the town of Peterhof. The station in Alexandria served not only the court, but also the whole town, with a public telegraph office for the local residents. The palace telegraph station was designed by Andrei Stakenschneider. In keeping with

The operations room

A telegraph worker. 1868

The ice-house

The Farm Palace

IN THE LATE 1820s, on Nicholas I's orders, the Alexandria ensemble was enlarged with a small elegant pavilion adjoining the Farm built by Adam Menelaws. The rooms in the pavilion were intended as a summer residence for the young heir to the throne, the future Alexander II. In time the building was reconstructed. Before the Tsesarevich's wedding it was enlarged by Andrei Stakenschneider and by the 1850s it had become the grand Farm Palace, the family home of Emperor Alexander II. The complex included Empress Maria Alexandrovna's Private Garden laid out on the east side to the design of the architect Eduard Hahn. This small area with a lawn and flowerbeds is enclosed by a pergola. In the centre is a fountain of *The Night*: in an oval

The Grotto Summerhouse. In the basin of the grotto – the *Boy and a Goose* sculpture. After a model by Ferdinand Hieronymus Schindler. 1854

Fountain with a statue of *The Night*. After an original
by Joseph-Michel-Ange Pollet. 1850s

Sculpture: *Girl with a Dog*
(*Innocence Protected by
Fidelity*). Sculptor: Giovanni
Maria Benzoni. 1863

basin surrounded by fine jets of water the bronze figure
of a naked girl floats connected to the pedestal only by
the clothing "slipping" off her. The fountain sculpture
was produced in the mid-1800s at the Chopin works
in St Petersburg from a cast of the marble original by
the French sculptor Joseph-Michel-Ange Pollet. In
the pergola itself there is one more fountain. This is
The Triumph of the Goddess of Beauty, a massive marble
bath into which jets pour from two lion's-head masks
attached to the adjacent pillars of the pergola. The
bath, made after a model by the architect and sculptor
Mikhail Shchurupov, is decorated with bas-reliefs of
classical gods and goddesses.

After coming to the throne in 1855, Alexander II
continued to enlarge the palace. A terrace appeared
on the east side connecting several rooms. The ground
floor contained the rooms of the Emperor and his wife,
Maria Alexandrovna. They were all finished in the
Gothic style. The largest and most precious interior
from an artistic point of view is the grandly imposing
Blue Study of Alexander II. It was created by Andrei
Stakenschneider. Blue drapery, light blue cloth on the
desks and oak furniture form an integrated ensemble in
this functional room, where the Emperor received his

Mask fountain

The Blue Study of Alexander II

The Drawing-Room of Empress Maria Alexandrovna

ministers and senior civil servants with their daily reports. The Blue Study retains the memory of important events for the state: it was within these walls that the "great reforms" of Alexander II's reign were planned, including the abolition of serfdom.

THE EMPRESS'S apartments – Drawing-Room, Study, Bedroom, Dressing-Room and others – are decorated with an elegance characteristic of Maria Alexandrovna. Her exquisite taste is reflected in everything here: in the collections of paintings adorning the rooms, in the porcelain, glass and bronze ornaments and the furnishings. These apartments preserve the memory too of the Empress's selfless nature, of the difficult course of her life, clouded by the death of her eldest son, Nikolai, in 1865, the succession of attempts on her husband's life and, finally, the breakdown of their relationship. Maria Alexandrovna quietly expired from consumption in May 1880. Less than a year later, on 1 March 1881, Alexander was killed by another group of assassins.

Maria Alexandrovna's Study

Chandelier. Germany. Late 18th century

Clock. Bronzesmith:
L. Hennert.
Germany(?).
1830s

Sculpture: *A Shepherdess and Her Cavalier*. From
a model by Johann Joachim Kändler. Meissen
Porcelain factory, Saxony, Germany. 1738

The Dining-Room

The Colonists' Park

AFTER MAKING a gift of Alexandria to his wife, Nicholas I continued construction work at Peterhof. South of the Upper Garden, on the site of the Hunting Marsh, he decided to create a picturesque pond with two small islands. The area became known as the Colonists' Park, because nearby were the houses of German settlers who had come from Württemberg. The work to create the park with an area of some 30 hectares was planned

by Stakenschneider and carried out under the direction of master gardener Peter Ehrler. It was in the main complete by 1848. A considerable part of the ensemble was occupied by Olga's Pond, named in honour of Grand Duchess Olga Nikolayevna, one of the Emperor's daughters. On the two islands in the pond Stakenschneider constructed the Tsarina's and Olga's Pavilions.

Column in the garden on Tsarina's Island.
Sculpture: *A Girl Feeding a Parrot with Grapes.*
After a model by Heinrich Berges. 1850s

View from the
Drawing-Room
into the Atrium

←
View of the Tsarina's Pavilion
from Olga's Pond

The Tsarina's Pavilion

THE ELEGANT building of the Tsarina's Pavilion is surrounded by a magnificent garden with fountains, statues and marble benches. In creating on the island a world of romantic dreams and fabulous illusions that was close to the Empress's heart, Stakenschneider made her a gift, as it were, of her own little corner of Italy. White Carrara marble predominated in the decoration of the island. Under the guidance of master gardener Ehrler the grounds were planted with limes, oaks, maples, ashes, lilacs, willows and chestnuts. One of the oaks was grown from an acorn brought from America, where it came from the tree above the grave of George Washington. The parterre in the centre of the island is adorned by a marble fountain basin over which Narcissus bends admiring his own reflection.

Laid out on the north side of the pavilion is the Private Garden, where elegant floral compositions set off the marble bases and capitals of columns in the centre of five flowerbeds. The chief attraction of the garden, though, is a column made of 30 tubes of blue and milk glass topped by a gilded sculpture of *A Girl Feeding a Parrot with Grapes.* The column was sent as a gift to Alexandra Feodorovna in 1854 by her brother, King Frederick William IV of Prussia.

Table with a mosaic *Views of Rome* top.
Italy. 19th century

The Dining-Room

The Study of Empress Alexandra Feodorovna

The Tsarina's Pavilion was constructed in 1842–44 to Stakenschneider's design in a "Pompeian" style. The architect, who had visited Pompeii, reproduced the appearance of an Ancient Roman house like those that had been uncovered in the excavation of the famous town buried beneath the volcanic ash of Vesuvius. The interior is finished with great refinement using intensely bright colours. The central room is the columned Atrium, the prototype for which was a Roman courtyard with a marble pool and fountain. The area is painted in the "Pompeian" style and filled with marble and bronze sculpture and bronze small plastic art. The Exedra, an invariable feature of a rich Pompeian house, was designed with three niches that contain elegant furniture – semicircular couches and little tables with curved legs. This section acquires particular elegance from the mosaic floor created by craftsmen from the Peterhof Lapidary Works. The Oikos drawing-room is finished with marble of various shades. The floor of the Dining-Room is adorned by a rare authentic Ancient Roman mosaic that Nicholas I acquired from the husband of his eldest daughter, Maria – Duke Maximilian of Leuchtenberg, the grandson of Josephine Beauharnais. It was part of the famous Malmaison collection that belonged to Napoleon's first wife. On display in the Dining-Room and Drawing-Room are items from the Coral and Etruscan Services, both specially made for the Tsarina's Pavilion at the Imperial Porcelain Factory in the 1840s.

Olga's Pavilion

THE PAVILION on Olga's Island was a gift to Olga Nikolayevna for her wedding in 1846 and was also designed by Stakenschneider. The tall building resembles the villas on the outskirts of Palermo, at one of which the Grand Duchess had accepted Prince Charles of Württemberg's proposal. The Emperor's wedding present was a sort of souvenir of that visit to Italy, a splendid reminder of it. The architectural elements of the pavilion – the loggia, terraces, balconies and pergolas – create a bright summery mood. Bas-reliefs on the facades, bust in niches and the original water spouts in the form of winged dragons give the pavilion an exceptionally attractive appearance enhanced by its watery surroundings.

The Dining-Room

The Study of Nicholas I

Portrait of Nicholas I.
Sculptor: Ivan Vitali

A pair of cups and saucers decorated with portraits of Nicholas I and
Alexandra Feodorovna. Batenin Factory, St Petersburg, Russia. 1826–30

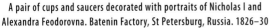

Each of the three floors contains just one large room – the Dining Room, Olga Nikolayevna's Study and Nicholas I's Study. They were exquisitely decorated by the painter Johann Drollinger and the sculptor Triscorni. The décor is complemented by authentic Russian-made furniture, paintings and items of everyday use. From the Study on the middle floor you can go out onto the balcony or terrace or descend an outside staircase to the garden. The roof of Olga's Pavilion was made into a viewing platform from which you can admire Peterhof's attractive surroundings.

The Study
of Olga Nikolayevna

A silver plate from Grand Duchess Olga
Nikolayevna's dowry. Made by Henrik August Long,
St Petersburg, Russia. 1840

Needlework box.
Russia. 1860s

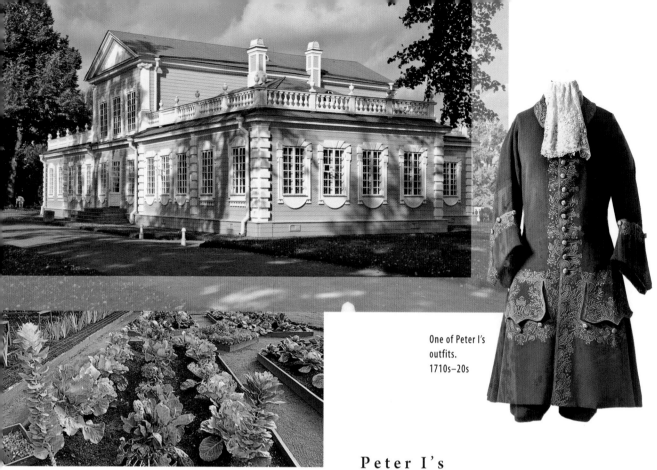

One of Peter I's
outfits.
1710s–20s

Peter's vegetable plot

Peter I's
Wayside Palace
at Strelna

AFTER RUSSIA recovered Ingermanland, Peter I's attention was taken by Strelna. He decided to use this convenient location to construct a suburban residence with fountains. Work began here on a small "wayside" palace and later on a grand residence. In 1715 construction was in full swing at Strelna: canals were dug, avenues were laid out and trees planted in the Upper and Lower Parks. Venetian specialists were engaged in hydrotechnical work under the direction of Vasily Tuvolkov, whom we have already met. In part due to him, Peter discovered the springs on the Ropsha Heights south of Peterhof and, realizing the potential of this water supply, rapidly cooled towards Strelna, becoming fired with the idea of Peterhof instead.

The Dressing-
Room

The Dining-Room

The Bedroom

The wooden palace at Strelna was nonetheless completed. The name of the original architect has been lost over the years, but we do know for certain that the building was erected by 1716 and reconstructed in 1719–20. It became the centre of a small estate with gardens, hothouses for exotic plants and Peter I's celebrated vegetable plot. It was here that that outlandish wonder the potato was first grown in Russia. In 1750, on Empress Elizabeth's orders, Francesco Bartolomeo Rastrelli carefully overhauled this precious relic of her father, replacing the rotten logs and laying new foundations.

The state rooms, administrative and living apartments of the building form a single complex filled with items of everyday use that accord with the purpose of the rooms and include quite a few directly connected with Peter I. They preserve the spirit of his time, allowing visitors to take themselves back to the complicated and contradictory era of the reformer Tsar. The small rooms of Peter's house are simple, comfortable and cosy. The walls are decorated with wood panelling, wallpaper or fabric. The largest room on the ground floor is the Dining-Room, divided into north and south sections by a mighty arch. The tea service for six with which the table is laid was made at the Meissen Porcelain Factory.

Oranienbaum

IN THE EARLY 1700s Peter I presented the site of the future Oranienbaum to his right-hand man, Alexander Menshikov. Here, on the furthest section of the Peterhof road, on the coast of the Gulf of Finland at the closest point to Kotlin Island, where he was overseeing the construction of Kronslot, the Illustrious Prince created his own estate. After Menshikov's fall from power in 1727 Oranienbaum had a succession of owners over the next two centuries. From the auspices of the Office of Works it passed to the Admiralty, then for almost twenty years from 1743 it was the residence of Grand Duke Peter Feodorovich, the future Emperor Peter III. After the palace coup of 28 June 1762,

The Great (Menshikov) Palace

Catherine II became the new mistress of Oranienbaum and she created the Private Dacha ensemble made up of unique Rococo style buildings here. The estate then passed to her grandchildren, first Emperor Alexander I and then, from 1831, to Grand Duke Mikhail Pavlovich. It was inherited by Mikhail's wife, Grand Duchess Yelena Pavlovna, who did much to help this astonishingly beautiful place to flourish. The last owners of Oranienbaum were her heirs, the Dukes of Mecklenburg-Strelitz. In the course of the 19th century such prominent architects as Carlo Rossi, Vasily Stasov, Andrei Stakenschneider and Harald Bosse contributed to the Oranienbaum estate.

Chandelier. Meissen
Porcleian Factory, Saxony,
Germany. Second half of
the 19th century

The Dining-Room

The Great (Menshikov) Palace

THE PALACES of Oranienbaum are unique. At a tremendous cost the defenders of the Oranienbaum pocket in the war years of 1941–44 saved the ensemble from destruction and today the palaces are the only ones in the suburbs of St Petersburg to have avoided the Nazi occupation and thus preserved their authenticity.

The Great Palace at Oranienbaum was created to the design of the Italian architect Francesco Fontana with input from Johann Gottfried Schädel and Johann Friedrich Braunstein. Through their efforts in the 1710s and '20s the core of the future palace-and-park complex was created – a magnificent ensemble that included the Lower Garden as well as the palace. A navigable canal led from the Gulf of Finland to the garden, ending in a small harbour. To the east of the palace the little River Karost was dammed to form the picturesque Lower Pond.

The Crimson Drawing-Room

The Large Study

Inside the Great Palace reflects its repeated changes of owner with features from various periods. The rooms on the upper floor acquired their present appearance in the 1850s, when they were refurbished for Grand Duchess Yelena Pavlovna in the "Second Rococo" style. Exquisite stuccowork, pastel colours and the absence of ponderous formal grandeur combine to give the rooms refinement and a certain affinity with the halls of those 18th-century masterpieces, the Chinese Palace and the Coasting Hill Pavilion.

The Ballroom

Display case in the Crimson Drawing-Room. Russia. Second half of the 19th century

The Picture House

The Picture House
and the "Stone Hall" pavilion

AFTER the marriage of the heir to the throne, Peter Feodorovich, and Sophie Friederike Auguste of Anhalt-Zerbst
(the future Catherine II) in 1745, Oranienbaum became the
summer residence of their "lesser court". To set the estate in
order, Empress Elizabeth sent Francesco Bartolomeo Rastrelli
here in the late 1740s and he reconstructed the Great Palace.
He probably also constructed the Picture House that housed
a collection of paintings, a chamber of curiosities and an opera
hall. At roughly this same time, in 1749–51, Oranienbaum acquired an amusement pavilion called the "Stone Hall" containing a large room with a stage. This building has been attributed
to both Rastrelli and Mikhail Zemtsov. The Triple Lime Alley
laid out from the pavilion in the 1750s later became a central
feature of Catherine II's Private Dacha.

The "Stone Hall"

Peterstadt

BY THE EARLY 1750s Rastrelli was busy on other projects and he was replaced at Oranienbaum by Antonio Rinaldi, who arrived in St Petersburg in 1751. In the late 1750s and early 1760s, together with the master mason Martin Hofmann, he built on the right bank of the Karost where the river entered the Great Pond a "toy" fortress – Peterstadt – for the heir to the throne, Peter Feodorovich. The centre of the star-shaped complex of elaborate bastions was a small two-storey palace in the Rococo style. The fortress also contained an arsenal, houses for the commandant and officers, a powder magazine and a Lutheran church. The garrison consisted of officers and men from Peter's native Holstein. A small garden for the fortress was laid out on the riverbank.

Like its master, Peterhof suffered a tragic fate and today the only reminders of this fascinating caprice of the unfortunate Emperor are the entrance gate and the Palace of Peter III.

The Round Hall in the Coasting-Hill Pavilion

The Coasting Hill

THE COASTING HILL was once a tremendous piece of architecture and engineering extending for some 530 metres. This early rollercoaster had three tracks over six metres wide. Special wheeled cars hurtled down the central one, while the outside two were used to return them to the top. With time, however, the tracks fell into disrepair and they were finally dismantled by 1861. Today all that survives of this unique structure is the enchantingly beautiful pavilion created by Antonio Rinaldi. Its interiors are striking for their extremely rare 18th-century artificial marble floors and the decorative painting of the walls and ceilings.

The Entrance Gate of the Peterstadt fortress

The Palace of Peter III

THIS ELEGANT two-storey palace, Rinaldi's first independent project in Russia, has to a large extent retained its original appearance. It was not intended for formal receptions: the ground floor contained service rooms, while above there were small ornate apartments. Paintings, lacquer panels, fabrics and woodcarving make their décor rich and varied.

The Pantry

Lacquer decorative painting. Artist: Feodor Vlasov. 1760s

Portrait of Peter III. Unknown artist. 1760s

Chandelier in the Picture Hall

The Picture Hall in the Palace of Peter III

The Chinese Palace

AFTER OVERTHROWING Peter III, Empress Catherine II commissioned Rinaldi to create the Private Dacha ensemble to the west of the Great Palace. Its main structure would be the incomparable Chinese Palace standing on the edge of a pond. The restrained treatment of the facades does not promise a particularly sumptuous interior. However, the decoration of the rooms combines a striking variety of decorative materials, exquisite stuccowork details, ceiling paintings created specially for the palace and many other Rococo elements. The most famous room is the Buglework Cabinet with embroidered panels of silk and bugles (tubular glass beads) made by nine Russian needlewomen under the direction of the Frenchwoman Marie de Chelles. The Chinese palace is a Rococo-style architectural monument unique for Russia and of exceptional artistic value.

The Blue Drawing-Room

Italian Landscape. Artist: Francesco Zuccarelli. 1750s

Ceiling painting in the Buglework Cabinet:
Fortune and Envy. Artist: Gasparo Diziani. 1760s

The Buglework Cabinet

The Hall of the Muses

Detail of a buglework panel

Peterhof's New Museums

OVER RECENT decades historical 19th-century buildings that formed part of the architectural ensemble of the Peterhof residence have undergone restoration. The creation of these museums was prompted by a desire to present Peterhof more fully as a place of summertime relaxation for the imperial dynasty. These permanent exhibitions located alongside the historical palaces and pavilions have become known as "the new museums".

A hall in the museum

Portrait of Maria Pavlova-Benois. Artist: Zinaida Serebriakova. 1923

An illustration for Walter Scott's novel *Quentin Durward*. Artist: Alexander Benois. 1890

The Benois Family Museum

THE FOUNDER of a creative dynasty that made an outstanding contribution to the development of Russian artistic culture was the confectioner Louis Jules Auguste César Benois, who was among the émigrés who fled the French Revolution. His son, Nikolai Leontyevich, and grandson, Leonty, became important architects. Another grandson, Alexander, was an art historian, an erudite critic, painter, graphic artist and theatrical designer, who proudly called himself "the product of an artistic family". His son, Nikolai Alexandrovich, became a theatrical artist and was for 35 years the chief designer at La Scala in Milan. Other creative relatives of the Benois family include the Lancerays, Serebriakovs, Tamanians and Schreters.

Many members of the Benois clan assisted in the creation of the museum whose displays tell the story of an amazingly gifted family inseparably connected with Peterhof. Its rooms contain works of painting, graphic art and sculpture, photographs and personal belongings.

The Western House for Maids-of-Honour

Harlequinade dish.
From a drawing
by V. Mosiagin. 1922

A hall in the museum

Katiusha on a Blanket.
Artist: Zinaida Serebriakova.
1920s

The Upper Garden House

The Museum of Collectors

THE DISPLAY of this museum, housed in the Upper Garden House, consists of the collections of prominent St Petersburg collectors donated by them to the State Museum Preserve. The collection of porcelain assembled by Iosif Ezrakh is unrivalled in private hands in Russia and includes first-rate pieces from all the key European factories in the 18th and 19th centuries. The collection of Roza and Alexander Timofeyev is represented primarily by paintings by Mstilav Dobuzhinsky, Nikolai Roerich, Boris Kustodiev and other major artists of the early 20th century. The museum's stocks also include the collections of A.V. Usenina (furniture, porcelain from private Russian factories), I.V. Kovarskaya (porcelain) and Yury Varshavsky (engraved portraits; displayed in the Benois Family Museum). The first-class works on show in the Museum of Collectors allow visitors to Peterhof to broaden their conceptions of the history of Russian and Western European art.

A model of Peter I's snow *Munker*. Made by marine engineer V. Krainiukov. 2003

The Imperial Yacht *Derzhava* in the Open Sea. Artist: A. Bobrov. 1901

The Imperial Yachts Museum

THIS MUSEUM tells of the history of Peterhof as the summer maritime residence of the Russian emperors. It had a specially equipped harbour used for mooring the imperial yachts that were on the rolls of the Russian navy. The display presents items of everyday use at sea. Here you can see Peter I's naval greatcoat, table services from the yachts, photographs and models of the vessels that served as "floating imperial residences". Particular attention is devoted to the largest and most advanced ocean-going yacht, the *Shtandart*, on board which Nicholas II received foreign heads of state. The King of Siam, the German Kaiser and the French President were here on brief diplomatic visits.

Emperor Nicholas II's family aboard the yacht *Shtandart*. 1906 photograph

The museum building

Items from the formal table service of the yacht *Livadia*. Designed by Ippolito Monighetti. 1871–73

A hall of the museum

The Museum of Fountain-Making

THIS MUSEUM, which opened in 2013 in the eastern gallery of the Great Palace, is devoted to a very important component of the Peterhof ensemble – its fountains. Behind their striking beauty lies a tremendous hydraulic complex: 135 engineering structures, more than 40 ponds, 56 kilometres of conduits and more, making up a unique gravity-driven system. The history of this complex is covered in detail in the museum display, currently the most modern in Peterhof, making extensive use of multimedia technology. Here, besides the traditional museum exhibits (sections of pipes, fountain jets, models of sculptural groups, firework patterns and other unique items), there are plasma panels presenting archive documents, technical drawings, photographs and animated diagrams that help visitors to understand the workings of the water supply to the Peterhof fountains.

Tools and utensils displayed in the museum: caulkers, a fountain spanner, skimmer and ladle for melting and pouring lead, and others

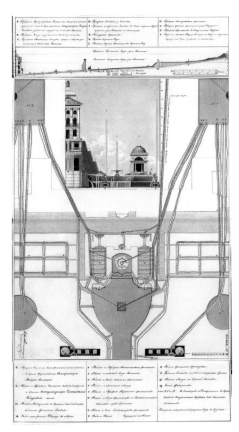

Drawing of the water supply for the Great Cascade and fountains of the Great Parterres. From an album by F. von Wistinghausen. 1824

A hall in the museum

The Playing Card Museum

THIS MUSEUM, which tells the history of playing cards, one of humanity' most enduring passions, was created on the basis of Alexander Perelman's collection numbering more than 40,000 items. For over three decades Perelman collected cards from all over the world. Outstanding among them are the original designs produced from the 17th century onwards by eminent artists in Europe, America, Asia and Russia. The display includes traditional playing cards, tarot and fortune-telling packs, children's, educational and other variants. Of particular interest is the pack of cards created by Adolphe Charlemagne, an academician of the Academy of Arts, His design has been in use in Russia for over 150 years now. Apart from the cards themselves, visitors can view card playing accessories and a large variety of items that shed light on the place of playing cards in human culture worldwide.

Playing cards

1. For the game of trapola
2. Historical. 19th century
3. With a military theme. 1880s
4. Anti-Fascist. 1941
5. Card Joke (transformation)
6. New Figures. 1860s
7. Travelling. 1860s

TEXT BY YELENA KALNITSKAYA

SCHOLARLY SUPERVISION OF THE PROJECT: P. KOTLIAR

TRANSLATOR: P. WILLIAMS

EDITOR: T. LOBANOVA

LAYOUT AND DESIGN: A. LOBANOV

PHOTOGRAPHERS: V. DAVYDOV, V. DENISOV, N. GONCHAROVA,

A. KASHNITSKY, V. KOROLEV, A. LOBANOV, A. PETROSIAN,

V. SAVIK, G. SEMENOV, G. SHABLOVSKY

MAP ARTIST: A. SMIRNOV

COLOUR CORRECTION: A. ILLARIONOV

Materials from the collection of the Peterhof State
Museum Preserve have been used in this publication.

*The Golden Lion publishing house thanks the staff of the Peterhof
State Museum Preserve for their assistance in preparing this album.*

ГОСУДАРСТВЕННЫЙ МУЗЕЙ-ЗАПОВЕДНИК
ПЕТЕРГОФ

GOLDEN
LION

© GOLDEN LION PUBLISHING HOUSE, 2014
Ulitsa Mira, 3, St Petersburg, 197101, Russia
Tel./Fax +7 (812) 493 5207

Printed in Russia